SCIENCE EXPLORER

MINERALS

SUPER COOL SCIENCE EXPERIMENTS: MINERALS

by Sophie Lockwood

CHERRY LAKE PUBLISHING • ANN ARBOR, MICHIGAN

A NOTE TO PARENTS AND TEACHERS: Please review the instructions for these experiments before your children do them. Be sure to help them with any experiments you do not think they can safely conduct on their own.

A NOTE TO KIDS: Be sure to ask an adult for help with these experiments when you need it. Always put your safety first!

CHERRY LAKE Publishing

Published in the United States of America by
Cherry Lake Publishing
Ann Arbor, Michigan
www.cherrylakepublishing.com

Content Editor: Robert Wolffe, EdD,
Professor of Teacher Education,
Bradley University, Peoria, Illinois

Book design and illustration: The Design Lab

Photo Credits: Cover and page 1, ©Icholakov/Dreamstime.com; page 4, ©Buhantsov Alexey, used under license from Shutterstock, Inc.; page 9, ©iStockphoto.com/lissart; page 12, ©Carlos Caetano, used under license from Shutterstock, Inc.; page 16, ©John Lens/Alamy; page 19, ©Antti Sompinmäki, used under license from Shutterstock, Inc.; page 23, ©PHOTOTAKE Inc./Alamy; page 28, ©MY_NEW_ IMAGES, used under license from Shutterstock, Inc.

Library of Congress Cataloging-in-Publication Data
Lockwood, Sophie.
Super cool science experiments: minerals / by Sophie Lockwood.
p. cm.—(Science explorer)
Includes bibliographical references and index.
ISBN-13: 978-1-60279-524-2 ISBN-10: 1-60279-524-X (lib. bdg.)
ISBN-13: 978-1-60279-602-7 ISBN-10: 1-60279-602-5 (pbk.)
1. Minerals—Experiments—Juvenile literature. 2. Mineralogy—Juvenile literature. I. Title. II. Title: Minerals. III. Series.
QE365.2.L63 2010
549.078—dc22 2009004313

Cherry Lake Publishing would like to acknowledge the work of The Partnership for 21st Century Skills. Please visit *www.21stcenturyskills.org* for more information.

SCIENCE EXPLORER

MINERALS

TABLE OF CONTENTS

What Is a Mineral?

Crystals come in different shapes and sizes.

Scientists have identified nearly 3,000 minerals. These substances formed by nature can be *very* different from one another. The physical state of some minerals can change. Solid minerals may become liquids or gases. Minerals might be crystals, and they might not be. Some minerals, such as salt, dissolve in water. Some, like coal, can burn. And frozen water—ice—is also a mineral when it forms in nature. Of course, ice can melt! As you can see, it is hard to pin down exactly what a mineral is.

One thing we do know about minerals is that they have properties that can be tested. Testing the properties of a substance helps scientists identify what kind of mineral it is. Minerals have various levels of hardness. Many have crystal patterns that can be seen and changed. Some have color and shine, such as diamonds or rubies. Some minerals, when handled in a certain way, can produce light.

Scientists who study minerals are called **mineralogists**. You can be a mineralogist in your kitchen or workshop. You can do experiments with things you already have. If you collect some minerals to work with, you can do even more!

In this book, you'll learn to work and think like a mineralogist. You'll do experiments that are easy and fun. You'll even learn how to design your own experiments!

First Things First

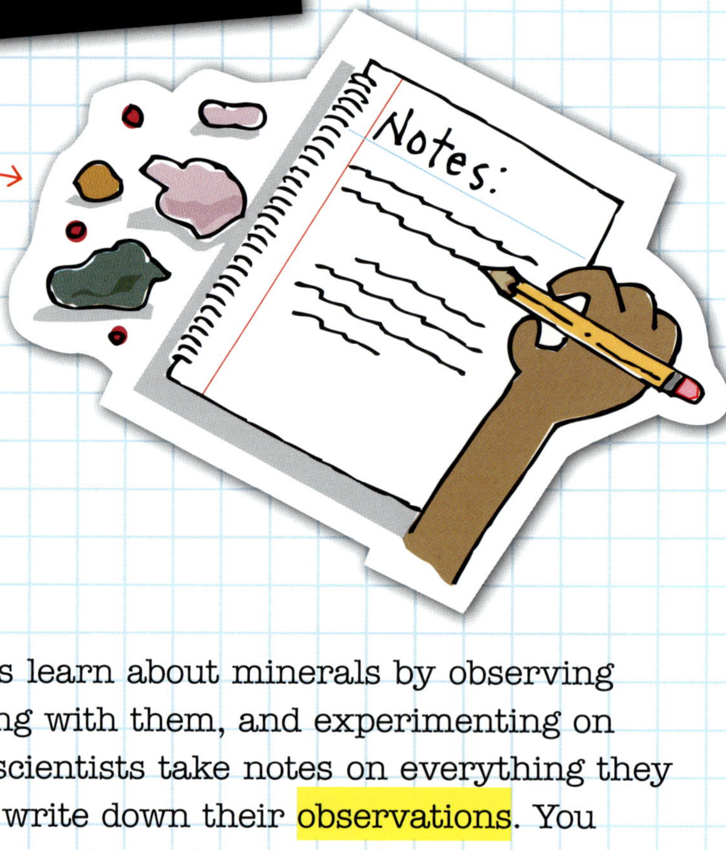

Mineralogists make careful notes about what they observe.

Mineralogists learn about minerals by observing them, working with them, and experimenting on them. Good scientists take notes on everything they notice. They write down their observations. You can do the same thing. As you work, write down everything you use, every step you take, what you see happening, and what you think the results mean.

When scientists design experiments, they must think very clearly. The way they think about problems is often called the scientific method. What is the scientific method? It's a step-by-step way of finding answers to specific questions. The steps don't always follow the same pattern. Sometimes scientists change their minds.

Scientific method

The process often works something like this:

- **Step One:** A scientist gathers the facts and makes observations about one particular thing.
- **Step Two:** The scientist comes up with a question that is not answered by all the observations and facts.
- **Step Three:** The scientist creates a hypothesis. This is a statement of what the scientist thinks is probably the answer to the question.
- **Step Four:** The scientist tests the hypothesis. He or she designs an experiment to see whether the hypothesis is correct. The scientist does the experiment and writes down what happens.
- **Step Five:** The scientist draws a conclusion based on how the experiment turned out. The conclusion might be that the hypothesis is correct. Sometimes, though, the hypothesis is not correct. In that case, the scientist might develop a new hypothesis and another experiment.

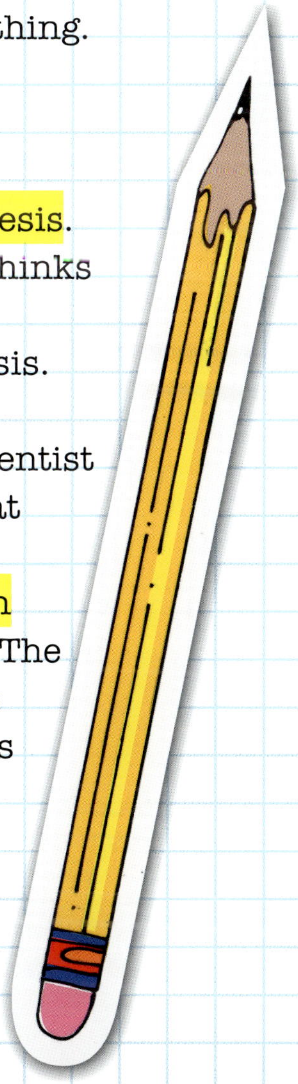

In the following experiments, you'll use the scientific method. You'll collect observations about minerals. For each experiment, you'll ask a question and develop a hypothesis. Then you'll do an experiment to see if your hypothesis is correct. Right or wrong, you will learn something about minerals.

For these experiments, you will need different minerals. There are many science supply stores and Web sites that sell mineral kits. Ask an adult to help you find a good one. Scientists, are you ready? Let's get started!

Your teacher might have a mineral kit you could borrow.

Experiment #1 How Hard Is It?

Rubies are red corundum.

One of the most important properties of minerals is hardness. Why would you want to know the hardness of a mineral?

Let's say you have a company that sells marble tile. You need to polish pieces of marble until they are smooth and shiny. To do so, you need a substance that is harder than marble. You would probably use corundum or diamond dust. These minerals are much harder than marble and will polish it so that it shines like clean glass.

Soft minerals, such as gypsum or talc, are sometimes ground up into baby powder. You can leave a mark on soft minerals with your fingernail. Slightly harder minerals, such as fluorite or calcite, can be marked with a knife blade. Very hard minerals can only be marked by diamonds!

Let's plan an experiment that tests mineral hardness. Start by gathering some information. You have probably seen and touched a piece of chalk at school. What did it feel like? Was it hard or soft? What about mica and quartz? For these, you will probably have to do a little research. What is mica used for? How about quartz? This information could give you clues about their hardness. Which of these three substances is the hardest? We need to make an educated guess based on what we know. Here is our hypothesis: **Quartz is harder than mica or chalk.**

Here's what you'll need:

- Pieces of chalk, mica, and quartz
- Your fingernail
- A nail file or a dinner knife

Be careful with the sharp tools!

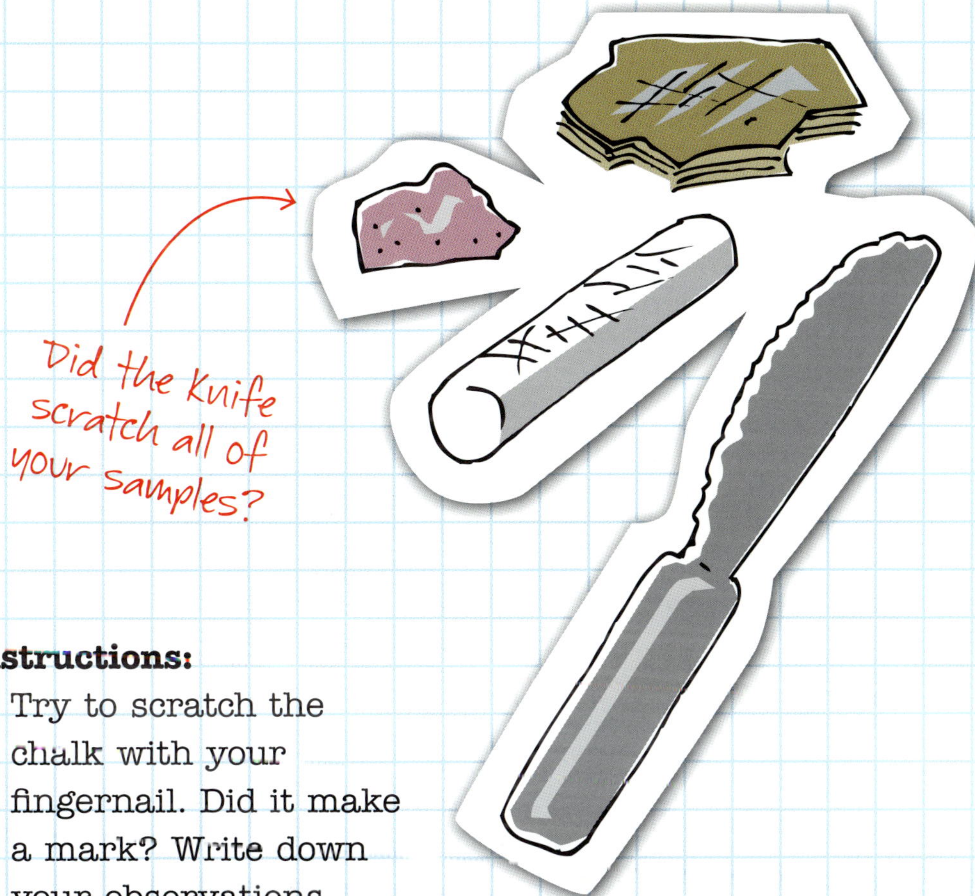

Instructions:

1. Try to scratch the chalk with your fingernail. Did it make a mark? Write down your observations.
2. Try to scratch the chalk with the nail file or dinner knife. Did it make a mark? Write down your observations.
3. Repeat steps 1 and 2 with the mica.
4. Repeat steps 1 and 2 with the quartz.

Conclusion:

What happened? The chalk and mica were easily scratched with your fingernail and the knife. The quartz was not. We proved our hypothesis—quartz is harder than chalk and mica. Wasn't that easy?

Experiment #2 Copper Cleaner

Air and the moisture in it react with iron to form rust.

Some minerals are metal. Gold, silver, copper, iron, and zinc are metals and minerals. Have you noticed that some metals change when exposed to air? Silver becomes dull and dark. Iron rusts. Copper develops a darker, brownish color. Do you think something besides air can change a mineral? Let's test copper and see if chemicals can change the appearance of this metallic mineral.

Here are two possible hypotheses:

Hypothesis #1: Acid will cause a chemical change in the appearance of copper.

Hypothesis #2: Acid will not cause a chemical change in the appearance of copper.

Select the hypothesis you think is correct. Now it is time to experiment!

Here's what you'll need:

- ¼ cup of lemon juice
- ½ cup of cider vinegar
- 1 teaspoon of salt
- A ceramic (glass or pottery) bowl
- A wooden spoon
- 10 very dirty pennies
- A pair of tweezers
- Paper towels
- Timer

Make sure you have everything before you begin your experiment.

Instructions:

1. Put the lemon juice, vinegar, and salt in the bowl. Stir the mixture with the wooden spoon until the salt is dissolved.
2. Hold a penny with the tweezers and dip it halfway into the liquid. Count to 20 and remove the penny. What did you observe? Write down your observations.
3. Place the remaining pennies in the liquid. Observe what happens over the next 5 minutes. Write down your observations.

4. Take 4 of the pennies out of the bowl. Place them on a folded sheet of paper towel. Do not rinse them off.
5. Remove the other 5 pennies. Rinse them in water and dry them. Lay the dry, clean pennies next to the unrinsed pennies on the paper towel. Set the timer for 20 minutes. Be sure to keep track of which pennies were rinsed and which were not.

Conclusion:

What happens to the unrinsed pennies? How does their appearance change? The mix of the acid liquid and the copper creates a new mineral, called malachite. What color is it? Write down your results. What can you conclude from this experiment? Was the hypothesis you chose correct?

Pennies are not pure copper because copper is expensive. U.S. pennies are made from an alloy, or mixture, of materials that is just 2.5 percent copper. The rest of the penny is zinc, a cheaper mineral. Even using cheaper metal, it costs 1.67 cents to make a penny. Making cents does not make sense!

Experiment #3
Sparks Fly

Why do you think they call it milky quartz?

A really cool property of some minerals is that they light up or glow! The word used to describe this light is triboluminescence. Say that five times in a row!

Squeezing, rubbing, or crushing certain minerals produces triboluminescence. There are many types of minerals that give off light when they are exposed to the right conditions. Let's do an experiment to try to find the best way to produce light from a mineral known as milky quartz. Here's our hypothesis: **Crushing milky quartz will produce more light than rubbing two pieces of milky quartz together.**

Here's what you'll need:

- 2 egg-sized pieces of milky quartz
- A piece of aluminum foil
- Safety glasses
- A hammer

Don't try this experiment without safety glasses!

Instructions:

1. This experiment must be done in the dark. Get all your materials ready and arrange them in such a way that you can find them in the dark. Close the blinds or curtains on the windows. Turn off the lights.
2. Hold a piece of milky quartz in each hand. Rub the minerals against each other. What do you see? Record your observations.

3. Strike one piece of quartz against the other. What happens? Record your observations.

4. Place one piece of quartz on the aluminum foil. Put on the safety glasses. Strike the milky quartz with the hammer. What do you see?

Be careful not to smash your fingers with the hammer!

Conclusion:

Were you able to produce triboluminescence with the milky quartz? Did you produce more or brighter light when you crushed the quartz than when you rubbed the pieces together? Was your hypothesis correct? Write up the results of your experiment so it can be shared with others. Good scientists share their results and conclusions. That way, others can try the same experiment and see if they get the same results. They can also use what you learned to come up with new hypotheses to test.

Salt is a mineral, and so are some forms of ice. These substances have crystal structures just like quartz, gold, or diamonds. If you get a chance to look at salt or ice through a microscope, you will see the crystals.

Experiment #4 Growing Crystals

Do you ever sprinkle some salt crystals on your food?

Most gems—such as diamonds, emeralds, and rubies—are minerals. Like ice and salt, they are also crystals. Their crystal structures are not easy to see with the human eye, but they do exist. They can be seen through a microscope.

You also know that diamonds are made from carbon. Have you ever seen a diamond in a piece of jewelry? Many times, diamond crystals are colorless. But can carbon produce crystals of different colors? Let's try using the carbon in charcoal briquettes to make colorful crystals. You will need an adult helper to do this project. Here is the hypothesis: **The carbon in charcoal briquettes can be used to produce colorful crystals.**

Here's what you'll need:

- Aluminum foil
- 4 charcoal briquettes (plain, without starter fluid)
- Vegetable food coloring (4 colors)
- A tablespoon
- Laundry bluing
- Iodized table salt
- A small bottle of ammonia (unscented)
- A small glass jar
- A plastic spoon for stirring

Be careful when handling the ammonia. It has strong fumes.

Instructions:

1. Tear off a piece of aluminum foil, about 12 inches (30 centimeters) square. Fold each side up about 1 inch (2.5 cm) to make a box.
2. Place 4 briquettes in the aluminum foil box. Place 3 or 4 drops of food coloring on each briquette. Use a different color for each briquette.
3. Have an adult help you carefully measure 2 tablespoons each of laundry bluing, salt, and ammonia and place them into a small glass jar. Do not breathe in the ammonia. Stir the mixture with a plastic spoon.
4. Pour some of the mixture over each briquette. What happens? Write down what you observe.

Conclusion:

What did you see? When the chemicals mix together, they interact with one another. The salt, which is a mineral crystal to begin with, combines with the other chemicals to create new crystals. What can you conclude from this experiment? Write up your experiment. Be sure to include your hypothesis, your materials, and the instructions. You want other scientists to be able to do the experiment exactly the way you did it. Write down your observations, and don't forget to include your conclusion!

Some of the world's largest crystals are found in the Naica lead, zinc, and silver mine in Chihuahua, Mexico. Crystals of gypsum or selenite as large as 4 feet (1.22 meters) across and 50 feet (15.2 m) long fill two huge chambers in part of the mine. The combined chambers are called the Crystal Cave of Giants.

Experiment #5 Specific Gravity

Which is the most dense—the water, the oil, or the cork?

Specific gravity is a measure of the density of a mineral compared to the density of water. Picture two minerals that are the same size. If one has more mass, it is denser. Why would you want to know about the density of a mineral?

Suppose someone gave you a piece of metal ore and said it was gold. If you know the specific gravity of gold, you can test the ore to see if it is really gold or just pyrite. Pyrite is a mineral that looks so much like gold that it is often called "fool's gold."

To find out the specific gravity of a sample, you need to know how much the sample weighs and the weight of the amount of water it displaces. If something displaces water, it pushes it out of the way. Let's do an experiment to determine the specific gravity of three mineral samples. To develop your hypothesis, predict **which of your three mineral samples will have the highest specific gravity**. Your prediction is your hypothesis!

Don't forget to write down your measurements!

Here's what you'll need:

- A 500-ml measuring cup
- Food scale (in grams)
- A 2-liter plastic soda bottle
- Scissors
- A one-hole paper punch
- A flexible drinking straw
- Small amount of modeling clay
- Water
- 3 different mineral samples, each about the size of a small egg
- String

Instructions:

1. Weigh the measuring cup using the food scale and record its weight in grams. Have an adult help you cut off the top of the soda bottle using the scissors, to form a cup about 4 inches (10 cm) deep.

2. Using the paper punch, punch a hole in the soda bottle about 1 inch (2.5 cm) from the top. Insert the flexible end of the straw into the hole, and seal the straw in place from the outside with the modeling clay. About ½ inch (1.5 cm) of the straw should be sticking into the soda bottle. Place the measuring cup next to the soda bottle, and put the other end of the straw in the measuring cup.
3. Pour water into the soda bottle until a small amount of water flows through the straw. Empty the extra water from the measuring cup. Be careful not to bump the bottle while you do so. Return the measuring cup to its position next to the soda bottle with the straw inside.

4. Weigh each mineral sample on the food scale. Record the number of grams each sample weighs.
5. Tie a piece of string around your first mineral sample. Lower it into the water. When it reaches the bottom, rest the string along the edge of the bottle. The water the mineral displaces will flow into the measuring cup. When the water stops flowing, weigh the measuring cup with the water in it. Write down the number. Subtract the weight of the empty cup from the weight of the cup with the water. Your answer will be the weight of the water.
6. Refill the soda bottle and repeat the process with the other two minerals. Record the weight of the displaced water for each mineral.
7. Find the specific gravity for each mineral sample. Use the following formula: specific gravity = mass (weight) of the rock in grams ÷ weight of the displaced water in grams. Here is an example: Specific gravity = 200 grams of rock ÷ 75 grams of displaced water. The specific gravity equals 2.67.

Conclusion:

Which mineral sample had the highest specific gravity? Which had the lowest? Was your hypothesis correct?

Experiment #6 Do It Yourself!

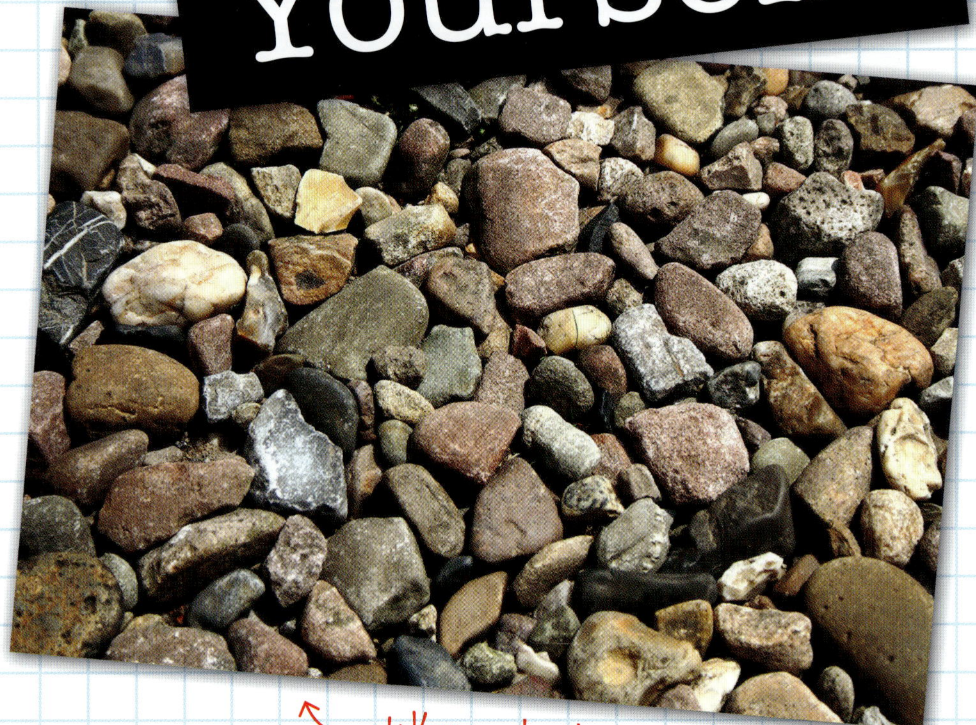

Why not start collecting rocks?

Ordinary rocks are made up of different types of minerals. You can test the specific gravity of rocks to help determine what they are made of. A rock with a low metal content should have a low specific gravity (1 to 2.5). A rock that contains heavier metals such as iron, lead, or silver might have a specific gravity of 4.5 or higher.

Collect some rock samples and determine their specific gravity. Follow each step of the scientific method. What is your hypothesis? What do you need to do your experiment? How will you perform the experiment? What do you observe? What is your conclusion? Write everything down.

You've done the experiments. You've learned about minerals. You know how to think and work like a mineralogist. Do you want to be a scientist when you grow up? Guess what? You don't have to wait until you grow up—you're an experienced scientist already!

GLOSSARY

alloy (AL-loy) a mixture of two or more metals

conclusion (kuhn-KLOO-zhuhn) a final decision, thought, or opinion

corundum (kuh-RUN-duhm) a very hard mineral

crystals (KRIS-tuhlz) mineral solids with a patterned structure and, often, flat outside surfaces

hypothesis (hy-POTH-uh-sihss) a logical guess about what will happen in an experiment

metallic (meh-TAL-lik) having metal content

method (METH-uhd) a way of doing something

mineralogists (min-uh-ROL-uh-jistss) people who study minerals

observations (ob-zur-VAY-shuhnz) things that are seen or noticed with one's senses

structures (STRUHK-shuhrz) the arrangements or ways in which parts of something come together, such as in crystals

triboluminescence (try-boh-loo-muh-NESS-uhns) light produced by pressure or by rubbing things together, usually from crystals

FOR MORE INFORMATION

BOOKS

Casper, Julie Kerr. *Minerals: Gifts from the Earth.* New York: Chelsea House, 2007.

Gardner, Robert. *Smashing Science Projects About Earth's Rocks and Minerals.* Berkeley Heights, NJ: Enslow Elementary, 2007.

Walker, Sally M. *Minerals.* Minneapolis, MN: Lerner Publications, 2007.

WEB SITES

A to Z Home's Cool Homeschooling—Rocks & Minerals

homeschooling.gomilpitas.com/explore/rocks.htm

An array of kid-friendly experiments

Rockhounding Arkansas—Experiments in Growing Crystals

rockhoundingar.com/pebblepups/growcryst.html

Several experiments to grow crystals

Rocks and Minerals

www.teachers.ash.org.au/jmresources/rocks/links.html

Information, activities, experiments, guides on how to identify rocks, and links to Web sites about minerals

INDEX

About the Author

In addition to writing books, Sophie Lockwood does experiments in her kitchen all the time! Although most of the experiments are called dinner, Sophie and her granddaughter actually did every experiment in this book. Sophie lives in South Carolina with her husband and enjoys reading, playing bridge, and watching movies when she isn't writing.